Coffee Recipes
Ground Coffee Goodness

by
Robert Hoffman

https://www.Kabsanka.com

Copyright © 2023

All Rights Reserved

This eBook is licensed for your enjoyment only. No rights are given to reselling this eBook. Enjoy the ground coffee recipes with your new machine.

INTRODUCTION

Welcome to "100 Recipes of Coffee" by Robert Hoffman, your ultimate guide to the world of coffee brewing! If you're a coffee lover, you know that there's nothing quite like the perfect cup of coffee to start your day off right. With this ebook, you'll have access to a variety of delicious and unique coffee recipes, from classic drip coffee to decadent lattes and everything in between. Robert Hoffman, a seasoned barista and coffee enthusiast, has carefully curated this collection of 100 coffee recipes to help you explore the wonderful world of coffee. Whether you're looking to try something new, impress your friends with your barista skills, or simply enjoy a delicious cup of coffee at home, you'll find something to suit your taste buds in this ebook. With step-by-step instructions and beautiful photos, "100 Recipes of Coffee" is the perfect companion for anyone who wants to learn more about coffee and take their brewing skills to the next level. So grab a cup of your favorite coffee, sit back, and enjoy the journey through the rich and diverse world of coffee with Robert Hoffman's 100 Recipes of Coffee.

TABLE OF CONTENT

Chapter 1: Classic Coffee Recipes

1. Espresso Shot
2. Americano
3. Latte
4. Cappuccino
5. Mocha
6. Macchiato
7. Flat White
8. Irish Coffee
9. Cortado
10. Affogato

Chapter 2: Cold Coffee Recipes

11. Iced Coffee
12. Cold Brew
13. Nitro Cold Brew
14. Frappuccino
15. Iced Latte
16. Iced Mocha
17. Iced Americano
18. Iced Caramel Macchiato
19. Vietnamese Iced Coffee
20. Bulletproof Coffee

Chapter 3: Seasonal Coffee Recipes

21. Pumpkin Spice Latte
22. Peppermint Mocha
23. Eggnog Latte
24. Gingerbread Latte
25. Cinnamon Roll Latte
26. Apple Cider Coffee
27. Hot Buttered Rum Coffee
28. Spiced Chai Latte
29. Chestnut Praline Latte
30. Maple Pecan Latte

Chapter 4: Non-Dairy Coffee Recipes

31. Almond Milk Latte
32. Soy Milk Cappuccino
33. Coconut Milk Mocha
34. Oat Milk Latte
35. Hemp Milk Coffee
36. Cashew Milk Cappuccino
37. Macadamia Nut Latte
38. Pea Milk Mocha
39. Rice Milk Latte
40. Sunflower Seed Milk Coffee

Chapter 5: Boozy Coffee Recipes

41. Baileys Irish Cream Coffee
42. Kahlua Coffee
43. Brandy Alexander Coffee
44. Irish Coffee Martini
45. Spiked Pumpkin Spice Latte
46. Whiskey Coffee
47. Chocolate Raspberry Martini Coffee
48. Espresso Martini
49. Vanilla Vodka Latte
50. Bourbon Caramel Latte

TABLE OF CONTENT

Chapter 6: Unique Coffee Recipes

51. Coffee Colada
52. Coffee Sangria
53. Coffee Smoothie
54. Coffee Milkshake
55. Chocolate Covered Cherry Coffee
56. Coffee Julep
57. Blueberry Coffee
58. Coffee Margarita
59. Lemon Coffee
60. Lavender Honey Latte

Chapter 7: International Coffee Recipes

61. Turkish Coffee
62. Greek Frappe
63. Italian Bicerin
64. Spanish Cafe con Leche
65. French Cafe au Lait
66. Moroccan Spiced Coffee
67. Vietnamese Egg Coffee
68. Ethiopian Coffee Ceremony
69. Indian Masala Chai
Mexican Cafe de Olla

Chapter 8: Keto Coffee Recipes

71. Bulletproof Coffee with MCT Oil
72. Butter Coffee
73. Coconut Oil Coffee
74. Turmeric Coffee
75. Cinnamon Coffee
76. Matcha Latte with Coconut Oil
77. Vanilla Almond Milk Latte
78. Keto Mocha
79. Cocoa Butter Coffee
80. Spiced Keto Coffee

Chapter 9: Gourmet Coffee Recipes

81. Maple Bacon Latte
82. Black Forest Mocha
83. White Chocolate Raspberry Mocha
84. Lavender Mocha
85. Cardamom Latte
86. Rosewater Latte
87. Honey Lavender Latte
88. Hazelnut Praline Latte
89. Tiramisu Latte
90. Peanut Butter Cup Latte

Chapter 10: Coffee Desserts

91. Coffee Ice Cream
92. Coffee Pudding
93. Coffee Cake
94. Coffee Brownies
95. Coffee Cheesecake
96. Coffee Toffee
97. Vietnamese Iced Coffee
98. Iced Caramel Macchiato
99. Iced Americano Coffee
100. Iced Mocha

Chapter 1: Classic Coffee Recipes

RECIPE NO#01
ESPRESSO SHOT

Ingredients:

- 1-2 ounces of finely
- Ground coffee beans
- Filtered water
- Espresso machine

Instructions:

1. Begin by filling the espresso machine's water reservoir with filtered water and turn on the machine to allow it to heat up.
2. Grind 1-2 ounces of coffee beans to a fine consistency. It is important to use freshly roasted coffee beans for the best flavor and aroma.
3. Remove the portafilter from the espresso machine and add the ground coffee to it. Use a tamper to press down the coffee grounds firmly.
4. Place the portafilter back into the machine and lock it into place. Place a shot glass or espresso cup under the spout to catch the espresso.
5. Press the button or lever on the machine to start the extraction process. The espresso should start to flow into the cup within 25-30 seconds. The perfect espresso shot should have a rich, dark crema on top.
6. Once the shot is complete, turn off the machine and remove the portafilter.
7. Clean the portafilter and spout by rinsing them with water and wiping them dry with a clean cloth.
8. Enjoy the espresso shot as is, or use it as a base for other coffee drinks like cappuccinos or lattes.

Chapter 1: Classic Coffee Recipes

RECIPE NO#02
AMERICANO

Ingredients:

- 1 shot of espresso (approximately 1.5 fluid ounces)
- Hot water
- Optional: Milk, cream, or sugar to taste

Instructions:

1. Start by brewing a shot of espresso in your espresso machine. Make sure the shot is strong and concentrated, as this will be the base for your Americano.
2. Once the espresso shot is brewed, heat up some water in a separate kettle or pot. You'll want enough water to fill your serving cup or mug.
3. Pour the hot water into your serving cup or mug, leaving enough space for the espresso shot.
4. Add the espresso shot to the cup with the hot water. You can adjust the ratio of espresso to water based on your preferences, but a common ratio is 1:2 (one part espresso, two parts water).
5. Stir the espresso and hot water together to combine. If desired, you can add milk, cream, or sugar to taste.
6. Enjoy your freshly made Americano coffee!

Chapter 1: Classic Coffee Recipes

RECIPE NO#03
LATTE

Ingredients:

- 1/2 cup of strong brewed coffee or 2 shots of espresso
- 1 cup of milk (whole, 2%, skim, or non-dairy milk like almond or oat)
- 1 tablespoon of granulated sugar or sweetener of your choice (optional)
- Whipped cream (optional)

Instructions:

1. Start by brewing a strong cup of coffee or making two shots of espresso. You can use a French press, drip coffee maker, or espresso machine.
2. In a small saucepan, warm up the milk on medium-low heat. Make sure not to boil the milk. You can also use a milk frother or microwave to warm up the milk.
3. If you want to add some sweetness to your latte, add a tablespoon of sugar or sweetener of your choice to the warm milk and stir until it's dissolved.
4. Once the milk is warm and frothy, pour it into a mug. Hold back the foam with a spoon as you pour, but reserve a small amount of foam for later.
5. Pour the strong coffee or espresso into the mug with the milk.
6. Use a spoon to scoop out the foam you reserved earlier and place it on top of the latte.
7. You can also add whipped cream on top of the foam for an extra decadent treat.
8. Enjoy your delicious homemade latte coffee!

Chapter 1: Classic Coffee Recipes

RECIPE NO#04
CAPPUCCINO

Ingredients:

- 1 shot of espresso (1-2 ounces)
- 8 ounces of milk (whole or 2%)
- 1 tablespoon of sugar (optional)
- Cinnamon powder (optional)

Instructions:

1. Brew a shot of espresso using an espresso machine, following the machine's instructions.
2. While the espresso is brewing, heat the milk in a small saucepan over medium heat until it begins to steam.
3. Use a milk frother or a whisk to froth the milk. If using a milk frother, place the frother in the milk and turn it on until the milk becomes frothy. If using a whisk, whisk the milk vigorously in the saucepan until it becomes frothy.
4. Pour the hot espresso into a cappuccino cup.
5. Spoon the frothed milk over the espresso, holding back the foam with a spoon until the cup is about 2/3 full.
6. Use the spoon to add the foam on top of the milk. You can sprinkle some cinnamon powder on top if desired.
7. Serve immediately and enjoy your delicious cappuccino coffee!

Chapter 1: Classic Coffee Recipes

RECIPE NO#05
MOCHA

Ingredients:

- 1 shot of espresso
- 1 tablespoon of cocoa powder
- 1 tablespoon of granulated sugar
- 1/4 cup of milk
- Whipped cream (optional)

Instructions:

1. Brew a shot of espresso using an espresso machine or stovetop espresso maker.
2. In a small saucepan, combine the cocoa powder, granulated sugar, and milk. Heat the mixture over medium heat, stirring constantly, until the sugar has dissolved and the mixture is hot.
3. Pour the hot milk mixture into the espresso shot and stir to combine.
4. If desired, top with whipped cream and sprinkle with cocoa powder.

Enjoy your delicious homemade Mocha Coffee!

Chapter 1: Classic Coffee Recipes

RECIPE NO#06
MACCHIATO

Ingredients:

- 1 shot of espresso
- 1-2 teaspoons of caramel syrup
- 1-2 tablespoons of foamed milk
- Whipped cream (optional)

Instructions:

1. Brew a shot of espresso using an espresso machine or stovetop moka pot.
2. Pour 1-2 teaspoons of caramel syrup into a small coffee cup.
3. Pour the shot of espresso over the caramel syrup.
4. Using a milk frother or by heating milk on the stovetop and whisking vigorously, foam 1-2 tablespoons of milk until it becomes thick and creamy.
5. Spoon the foamed milk over the espresso and caramel mixture.
6. If desired, add a dollop of whipped cream on top.

Your Macchiato coffee is now ready to enjoy!

Chapter 1: Classic Coffee Recipes

Recipe No#07
Flat White

Ingredients:

- 1-2 shots of espresso
- 6-8 oz of milk (whole or skim)
- Steaming pitcher
- Milk frother or steam wand
- Espresso machine

Instructions:

1. Start by heating up your espresso machine and steaming pitcher, as well as the milk frother or steam wand.
2. While waiting for the machine to heat up, grind your coffee beans and prepare your espresso shots according to your preference.
3. Once the espresso shots are ready, pour them into your preheated steaming pitcher.
4. Next, use your milk frother or steam wand to steam and froth the milk. Place the steam wand just below the surface of the milk, with the tip slightly angled, and begin steaming.
5. As you steam, move the pitcher around to create a whirlpool effect and incorporate air into the milk, which will create the microfoam texture that is characteristic of a flat white.
6. Continue steaming until the milk reaches a temperature of around 140-160°F.
7. Once the milk is steamed and frothed to your desired texture, give it a quick swirl to incorporate any large bubbles that may have formed.
8. Pour the milk into your espresso shots, holding back the foam with a spoon. Pour the milk in a circular motion to create latte art or leave it plain, depending on your preference.
9. Enjoy your delicious flat white coffee! and frothing the milk.

Chapter 1: Classic Coffee Recipes

RECIPE No#08
IRISH COFFEE

Ingredients:

- 1 cup freshly brewed hot coffee
- 1 tablespoon brown sugar
- 1 1/2 ounces Irish whiskey
- Heavy cream, lightly whipped

Instructions:

1. Brew a cup of coffee and pour it into a preheated glass or mug.
2. Add one tablespoon of brown sugar and stir until dissolved.
3. Add 1 1/2 ounces of Irish whiskey and stir to combine.
4. Using a spoon, gently pour lightly whipped heavy cream over the back of the spoon onto the coffee mixture. The cream should float on top.
5. Optional: dust the top with a pinch of cocoa powder or cinnamon.

Enjoy your delicious Irish Coffee!

Chapter 1: Classic Coffee Recipes

RECIPE NO#09
CORTADO COFFEE

Ingredients:

- 1 shot of espresso
- 2 ounces of steamed milk
- Optional: sugar or sweetener to taste

Instructions:

1. Begin by brewing one shot of espresso. You can use an espresso machine or a moka pot to make the espresso.
2. Steam 2 ounces of milk using a steaming wand on an espresso machine or a separate milk frother. The milk should be heated to around 150-160°F (65-70°C) and should have a velvety texture.
3. Pour the steamed milk over the espresso shot. The ratio of espresso to milk in a cortado is typically 1:1 or 1:2, depending on your preference.
4. If desired, add sugar or sweetener to taste.
5. Enjoy your delicious cortado coffee!

Chapter 1: Classic Coffee Recipes

RECIPE NO#10
CORTADO COFFEE

Ingredients:

- 1 shot of espresso or 1/4 cup strong brewed coffee
- 1 scoop of vanilla ice cream
- Optional: whipped cream, chocolate shavings, or cocoa powder for garnish

Instructions:

1. Brew your espresso or strong coffee and let it cool slightly.
2. Place a scoop of vanilla ice cream into a serving glass.
3. Pour the hot espresso or coffee over the ice cream.
4. Garnish with whipped cream, chocolate shavings, or cocoa powder, if desired.
5. Serve immediately and enjoy your delicious Affogato coffee!

Chapter 2: Cold Coffee Recipes

RECIPE NO#11
ICED COFFEE

Ingredients:

- 1 cup of freshly brewed coffee, chilled
- 1 cup of ice cubes
- 1/2 cup of milk or cream
- 1-2 tablespoons of sweetener
- Whipped cream (optional)

Instructions:

1. Brew a cup of coffee using your preferred method. You can use any type of coffee you like, but make sure it's strong enough to stand up to the ice and milk.
2. Let the coffee cool to room temperature, then transfer it to a pitcher and place it in the refrigerator to chill for at least 30 minutes.
3. Once the coffee is chilled, fill a tall glass with ice cubes.
4. Pour the chilled coffee over the ice cubes, filling the glass about 3/4 of the way.
5. In a separate container, mix together the milk or cream and sweetener until the sweetener is dissolved.
6. Pour the milk mixture over the coffee and ice, filling the glass to the top.
7. Stir the coffee and milk mixture together until everything is well combined.
8. Top with whipped cream if desired.
9. Enjoy your delicious iced coffee!

Chapter 2: Cold Coffee Recipes

RECIPE NO#12
COLD BREW

Ingredients:

- 1 cup of coarsely ground coffee beans
- 4 cups of cold filtered water
- Optional: sweetener of your choice, milk, cream

Instructions:

1. Grind your coffee beans coarsely. This will help prevent over-extraction during the brewing process.
2. Combine the coffee grounds and water in a large pitcher or container. Stir gently to ensure that all of the coffee is wet.
3. Cover the container and let it sit at room temperature for 12-24 hours. The longer you let it steep, the stronger and more concentrated the coffee will be. You can adjust the brewing time based on your personal taste preferences.
4. Once the coffee has brewed, strain it through a fine-mesh sieve or a cheesecloth into another pitcher or container. You may need to strain it twice to remove all of the sediment.
5. Serve the cold brew coffee over ice. You can add milk, cream, or sweetener if desired.
6. Store any leftover cold brew coffee in an airtight container in the refrigerator for up to a week.

Enjoy your delicious cold brew coffee!

Chapter 2: Cold Coffee Recipes

RECIPE NO#13
NITRO COLD BREW

Ingredients:

- 1 cup of coarsely ground coffee
- 4 cups of cold water
- Nitrogen gas (either from a canister or from a nitrogen-infusing machine)
- Optional: sweetener or cream, to taste

Instructions:

1. Start by grinding the coffee beans coarsely. This will help the coffee extract slowly over time, giving it a smooth flavor.
2. Combine the coffee grounds and cold water in a large container or jar. Stir to ensure all the grounds are submerged in the water.
3. Cover the container or jar and let the mixture steep in the refrigerator for 12 to 24 hours. The longer it steeps, the stronger the coffee will be.
4. Once the coffee has finished steeping, strain it through a coffee filter or cheesecloth to remove the grounds.
5. Fill a tall glass with ice and pour the cold brew coffee over it, leaving about an inch of space at the top of the glass.
6. Now it's time to add the nitrogen. If you have a canister, simply attach it to the tap and release the nitrogen into the glass. If you have a nitrogen-infusing machine, follow the manufacturer's instructions to infuse the nitrogen into the coffee.
7. As the nitrogen is added, you should see a cascade effect and a creamy head forming on top of the coffee.
8. Once the nitrogen has been added, you can optionally add sweetener or cream to taste.
9. Give the coffee a quick stir and enjoy your smooth and creamy Nitro Cold Brew Coffee!

Chapter 2: Cold Coffee Recipes

RECIPE NO#14
NITRO COLD BREW

Ingredients:

- 1 cup of freshly brewed coffee, cooled
- 1/2 cup of milk
- 2 tablespoons of sugar
- 1 cup of ice
- Whipped cream (optional)

Instructions:

1. Begin by brewing a fresh cup of coffee. Once the coffee is brewed, set it aside to cool.
2. In a blender, add the cooled coffee, milk, sugar, and ice.
3. Blend the mixture on high speed until it becomes smooth and creamy.
4. Pour the frappuccino mixture into a tall glass.
5. Top with whipped cream, if desired.
6. Serve immediately and enjoy!

Chapter 2: Cold Coffee Recipes

RECIPE NO#15
ICED LATTE COFFEE

Ingredients:

- 1 cup strong brewed coffee
- 1/2 cup milk
- 1-2 tablespoons sugar or sweetener of your (optional)
- Ice cubes

Instructions:

1. Start by brewing your coffee. You can use a French press, drip coffee maker, or any other method you prefer. Make sure it's strong, as the ice will dilute it.
2. Let the coffee cool to room temperature. If you're in a hurry, you can put it in the fridge for a few minutes.
3. Once the coffee is cooled, pour it into a glass with ice cubes. Leave some space at the top for the milk.
4. In a separate container, froth the milk. You can use a milk frother, a whisk, or even a blender. The milk should be thick and creamy, with lots of small bubbles.
5. Pour the frothed milk over the coffee and ice. You can use a spoon to hold back the foam if you prefer.
6. If you like your latte sweetened, add sugar or sweetener to taste. Stir well.
7. Garnish your iced latte with a sprinkle of cocoa powder, cinnamon, or nutmeg if you like.
8. Enjoy your delicious iced latte coffee!

Chapter 2: Cold Coffee Recipes

RECIPE NO#16
ICED MOCHA

Ingredients:

- 2 shots of espresso (or 1/2 cup of strongly brewed coffee)
- 1 cup of milk
- 1/4 cup of chocolate syrup
- 1 tablespoon of sugar (optional)
- 1 cup of ice

Instructions:

1. Brew two shots of espresso or make 1/2 cup of strongly brewed coffee. Allow it to cool to room temperature.
2. In a separate glass, mix together 1/4 cup of chocolate syrup and 1 tablespoon of sugar (if using) until well combined.
3. Pour the cooled espresso or coffee over the chocolate mixture and stir until well combined.
4. Add 1 cup of ice to the mixture and pour in 1 cup of milk.
5. Stir everything together until well combined.
6. Taste and adjust the sweetness if necessary.
7. Pour the iced mocha coffee into a glass filled with ice.
8. Optional: Top with whipped cream and drizzle additional chocolate syrup over the top.
9. Enjoy your delicious iced mocha coffee!

Chapter 2: Cold Coffee Recipes

RECIPE NO#17
ICED AMERICANO

Ingredients:

- 2 shots of espresso
- 1 cup of cold water
I- Ice cubes
- Optional: sweetener and milk of your choice

Instructions:

1. Brew two shots of espresso using your preferred brewing method. You can use a coffee machine or a stovetop espresso maker.
2. Fill a tall glass with ice cubes.
3. Pour the brewed espresso over the ice.
4. Add a cup of cold water to the glass. You can adjust the amount of water according to your preference.
5. Stir the drink to combine the espresso, water, and ice.
6. Add sweetener or milk of your choice, if desired. You can use sugar, honey, or a flavored syrup as a sweetener, and milk, cream, or a dairy-free alternative for a creamier taste.
7. Serve immediately and enjoy your refreshing Iced Americano Coffee!

Chapter 2: Cold Coffee Recipes

RECIPE NO#18
ICED CARAMEL

Ingredients:

- 1 cup of cold milk
- 1 tablespoon of caramel sauce
- 1 shot of espresso
- Ice cubes

Instructions:

1. Brew two shots of espresso using your preferred brewing method. You can use a coffee machine or a stovetop espresso maker.
2. Fill a tall glass with ice cubes.
3. Pour the brewed espresso over the ice.
4. Add a cup of cold water to the glass. You can adjust the amount of water according to your preference.
5. Stir the drink to combine the espresso, water, and ice.
6. Add sweetener or milk of your choice, if desired. You can use sugar, honey, or a flavored syrup as a sweetener, and milk, cream, or a dairy-free alternative for a creamier taste.
7. Serve immediately and enjoy your refreshing Iced Americano Coffee!

Chapter 2: Cold Coffee Recipes

RECIPE NO#19
VIETNAMESE ICED

Ingredients:

- 2 tablespoons of coarsely ground dark roast coffee
- 2 tablespoons of sweetened condensed milk
- 1 cup of hot water
- Ice cubes

Instructions:

1. Start by brewing two tablespoons of coarsely ground dark roast coffee using a traditional Vietnamese coffee filter. If you don't have a filter, you can use a French press or a drip coffee maker.
2. Add two tablespoons of sweetened condensed milk to a tall glass.
3. Once the coffee has finished brewing, pour it into the glass with the condensed milk and stir until well combined.
4. Fill the glass with ice cubes.
5. Stir the drink again to ensure that the condensed milk and coffee are evenly mixed.
6. Serve and enjoy your homemade Vietnamese Iced Coffee!

Chapter 2: Cold Coffee Recipes

RECIPE NO#20
BULLETPROOF

Ingredients:

- 1 cup of freshly brewed coffee
- 1 tablespoon of grass-fed butter
- 1 tablespoon of MCT oil or coconut oil

Instructions:

1. Start by brewing one cup of high-quality coffee using your preferred brewing method.
2. Add the hot coffee to a blender.
3. Add one tablespoon of grass-fed butter to the blender.
4. Add one tablespoon of MCT oil or coconut oil to the blender.
5. Blend the ingredients on high for 30 seconds, or until the mixture is smooth and frothy.
6. Pour the mixture into a mug and enjoy your homemade Bulletproof Coffee!

Chapter 3: Seasonal Coffee Recipes

RECIPE NO#21
PUMPKIN SPICE

Ingredients:

- 1 cup of strong coffee or espresso
- 1 cup of milk
- 2 tablespoons of pumpkin puree
- 2 tablespoons of brown sugar
- 1/2 teaspoon of pumpkin pie spice

Instructions:

1. Start by brewing one cup of strong coffee or espresso using your preferred brewing method.
2. In a small saucepan, heat one cup of milk over medium heat until it starts to steam.
3. Add two tablespoons of pumpkin puree, two tablespoons of brown sugar, and 1/2 teaspoon of pumpkin pie spice to the milk. Whisk until the ingredients are well combined.
4. Pour the milk mixture into a blender and blend until the mixture is smooth and frothy.
5. Pour the coffee or espresso into a mug.
6. Pour the frothed milk mixture on top of the coffee or espresso.
7. Top with whipped cream and a sprinkle of pumpkin pie spice, if desired.
8. Enjoy your homemade Pumpkin Spice Latte!

Chapter 3: Seasonal Coffee Recipes

RECIPE NO#22
PEPPERMINT MOCHA

Ingredients:

- 1 cup of strong coffee or espresso
- 1/2 cup of milk
- 2 tablespoons of chocolate syrup
- 1/2 teaspoon of peppermint extract
- Whipped cream for topping (optional) + Candy

Instructions:

1. Start by brewing one cup of strong coffee or espresso using your preferred brewing method.
2. In a small saucepan, heat 1/2 cup of milk over medium heat until it starts to steam.
3. Add two tablespoons of chocolate syrup and 1/2 teaspoon of peppermint extract to the milk. Whisk until the ingredients are well combined.
4. Pour the coffee or espresso into a mug.
5. Pour the milk mixture on top of the coffee or espresso.
6. Top with whipped cream and a sprinkle of crushed candy canes, if desired.
7. Enjoy your homemade Peppermint Mocha!

Chapter 3: Seasonal Coffee Recipes

RECIPE NO#23
EGGNOG LATTE

Ingredients:

- 1 cup of eggnog
- 1 shot of espresso or 1/2 cup of strong brewed coffee
- 1/2 cup of milk
- 1/4 tsp of ground cinnamon
- Whipped cream (optional) + Ground nutmeg (optional)

Instructions:

1. Heat the eggnog in a small saucepan over medium heat until it starts to steam.
2. While the eggnog is heating, brew a shot of espresso or strong coffee.
3. Add the brewed espresso or coffee to a large mug.
4. Froth the milk using a milk frother or by heating it in a small saucepan and whisking vigorously until frothy.
5. Pour the heated eggnog and frothed milk into the mug with the espresso or coffee.
6. Stir in the ground cinnamon.
7. Top with whipped cream and a sprinkle of ground nutmeg, if desired.
8. Serve hot and enjoy your delicious Eggnog Latte!

Chapter 4: Non-Dairy Coffee Recipes

RECIPE NO#32
SOY MILK CAPPUNCCINO

Ingredients:

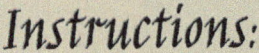

- 1 cup soy milk
- 1-2 shots of espresso or 1/2 cup brewed coffee
- sweetener of your choice (optional)

Instructions:

In a small saucepan, heat the soy milk over medium heat until it starts to steam. Do not let it boil.
While the milk is heating up, brew your espresso or coffee.
Once the milk is heated, pour it into a blender and blend on high for 15-20 seconds until it becomes frothy.
Pour the coffee into a large mug or cup.
Pour the frothy soy milk over the coffee, using a spoon to hold back the froth if necessary.
Spoon the froth on top of the coffee.
Add sweetener to taste if desired and stir.
Enjoy your delicious soy milk cappuccino coffee!

Chapter 3: Seasonal Coffee Recipes

RECIPE NO#24 GINGERBREAD LATTE

Ingredients:

- 1 shot of espresso or 1/2 cup of strong brewed coffee
- 1/2 cup of milk
- 1 tbsp of molasses
- 1/4 tsp of ground ginger
- 1/4 tsp of ground cinnamon + 1/8 tsp of ground nutmeg

Instructions:

1. Brew a shot of espresso or strong coffee.
2. In a small saucepan, heat the milk, molasses, ground ginger, ground cinnamon, and ground nutmeg over medium heat until it starts to steam.
3. Froth the milk using a milk frother or by heating it in a small saucepan and whisking vigorously until frothy.
4. Pour the brewed espresso or coffee into a large mug.
5. Pour the heated and frothed milk mixture over the espresso or coffee.
6. Top with whipped cream and a sprinkle of ground cinnamon or nutmeg, if desired.
7. Serve hot and enjoy your delicious Gingerbread Latte!

Chapter 3: Seasonal Coffee Recipes

RECIPE NO#25
CINNAMON ROLL

Ingredients:

- 1 shot of espresso or 1/2 cup of strong brewed coffee
- 1/2 cup of milk
- 1 tbsp of cinnamon syrup
- 1/2 tsp of vanilla extract
- Whipped cream (optional) + Ground cinnamon (optional)

Instructions:

1. Brew a shot of espresso or strong coffee.
2. In a small saucepan, heat the milk, cinnamon syrup, and vanilla extract over medium heat until it starts to steam.
3. Froth the milk using a milk frother or by heating it in a small saucepan and whisking vigorously until frothy.
4. Pour the brewed espresso or coffee into a large mug.
5. Pour the heated and frothed milk mixture over the espresso or coffee.
6. Top with whipped cream and a sprinkle of ground cinnamon, if desired.
7. Serve hot and enjoy your delicious Cinnamon Roll Latte!

Chapter 3: Seasonal Coffee Recipes

RECIPE NO#26
APPLE CIDER

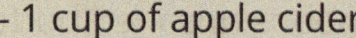

Ingredients:

- 1 cup of apple cider
- 1/2 cup of strong brewed coffee
- 1/4 cup of milk + 1/4 tsp of ground cinnamon
- 1/8 tsp of ground nutmeg
- Whipped cream (optional) + Cinnamon stick (optional)

Instructions:

1. Brew a strong cup of coffee and set aside.
2. In a small saucepan, heat the apple cider, milk, ground cinnamon, and ground nutmeg over medium heat until it starts to steam.
3. Froth the milk using a milk frother or by heating it in a small saucepan and whisking vigorously until frothy.
4. Pour the brewed coffee into a large mug.
5. Pour the heated and frothed apple cider mixture over the coffee.
6. Top with whipped cream and a cinnamon stick, if desired.
7. Serve hot and enjoy your delicious Apple Cider Coffee!

Chapter 3: Seasonal Coffee Recipes

RECIPE NO#27
HOT BUTTERED RUM

Ingredients:

- 1 cup strong brewed coffee + 2 tablespoons unsalted butter
- 1 tablespoon brown sugar
- 1/2 teaspoon ground cinnamon
- 1/4 teaspoon ground nutmeg + 1/4 teaspoon vanilla extract
- 1 ounce dark rum + Whipped cream (optional)

Instructions:

1. Brew a cup of strong coffee using your preferred method.
2. In a small saucepan, melt the butter over low heat.
3. Once the butter is melted, stir in the brown sugar, cinnamon, nutmeg, and vanilla extract. Cook the mixture for about 1-2 minutes, stirring occasionally, until the sugar is dissolved and the spices are fragrant.
4. Add the brewed coffee and rum to the saucepan and stir to combine. Heat the mixture over medium-low heat, stirring occasionally, until it's hot.
5. Pour the hot buttered rum coffee into a mug and top with whipped cream, if desired. You can also sprinkle a little extra cinnamon or nutmeg on top for added flavor.
6. Enjoy your delicious and cozy Hot Buttered Rum Coffee!

Chapter 3: Seasonal Coffee Recipes

RECIPE NO#28
SPICED CHAI LATTE

Ingredients:

1 shot of espresso (or 1/2 cup strong brewed coffee)
1 cup of milk
2 tablespoons of chestnut praline syrup
Whipped cream (optional)
Crushed chestnuts (optional)

Instructions:

1. In a small saucepan, heat the milk, ground cinnamon, ground ginger, ground cardamom, ground cloves, and ground black pepper over medium heat until it starts to steam.
2. Add the black tea bag to the milk mixture and let steep for 3-5 minutes, depending on how strong you like your tea.
3. Remove the tea bag and stir in honey or sugar, if desired.
4. Froth the milk using a milk frother or by heating it in a small saucepan and whisking vigorously until frothy.
5. Pour the spiced milk mixture into a large mug.
6. Top with whipped cream, if desired.
7. Serve hot and enjoy your delicious Spiced Chai Latte!

Chapter 3: Seasonal Coffee Recipes

RECIPE NO#29
CHESTNUT PRALINE

Ingredients:

- 1 shot of espresso (or 1/2 cup strong brewed coffee)
- 1 cup of milk
- 2 tablespoons of chestnut praline syrup
- Whipped cream (optional)
- Crushed chestnuts (optional)

Instructions:

1. Brew one shot of espresso (or 1/2 cup of strong brewed coffee).
2. Heat the milk in a saucepan over medium heat, stirring constantly, until it's hot but not boiling. Alternatively, you can use a milk frother to heat and froth the milk.
3. Add the chestnut praline syrup to the milk and stir well to combine.
4. Pour the espresso into a large mug, then pour the milk and syrup mixture over the espresso.
5. If desired, top with whipped cream and a sprinkle of crushed chestnuts.
6. Serve immediately and enjoy your delicious Chestnut Praline Latte!

Chapter 3: Seasonal Coffee Recipes

RECIPE NO#30
MAPLE PECAN

Ingredients:

- 2 cups milk
- 2 shots espresso (or 1/2 cup strong brewed coffee)
- 1/4 cup pecans, chopped
- 1/4 cup maple syrup + 1/2 tsp vanilla extract
- Whipped cream (optional)

Instructions:

1. In a small saucepan, heat the milk over medium-low heat until steaming hot. Do not boil.
2. While the milk is heating, prepare the espresso or strong brewed coffee.
3. In a small skillet, toast the chopped pecans over medium heat until lightly browned and fragrant. Remove from heat and set aside.
4. In a blender, combine the steamed milk, espresso or coffee, maple syrup, and vanilla extract. Blend on high speed until well combined and frothy.
5. Pour the maple pecan latte into two cups and sprinkle the toasted pecans on top.
6. If desired, top with whipped cream and an additional drizzle of maple syrup.

Chapter 3: Seasonal Coffee Recipes

RECIPE NO#31
ALMOND MILK LATTE

Ingredients:

- 1 cup unsweetened almond milk
- 1 shot of espresso or 1/2 cup of strong brewed coffee
- 1-2 teaspoons of honey (optional)
- Cinnamon powder (optional)

Instructions:

1. Start by heating the almond milk in a small saucepan over medium heat. Heat the milk until it's steaming hot but not boiling. You can also use a milk frother or microwave to heat the almond milk.
2. Once the almond milk is hot, pour it into a blender or use a hand frother to froth it until it's frothy and has a light foam on top.
3. Brew one shot of espresso or 1/2 cup of strong brewed coffee.
4. Add the brewed coffee to a large mug.
5. Pour the frothy almond milk over the coffee.
6. If desired, add 1-2 teaspoons of honey to sweeten the latte.
7. Sprinkle some cinnamon powder on top of the latte for added flavor and aroma.
8. Serve and enjoy your delicious and creamy almond milk latte coffee!

Chapter 4: Non-Dairy Coffee Recipes

RECIPE NO#32
SOY MILK CAPPUNCCINO

Ingredients:

- 1 cup almond milk
- 1-2 shots of espresso or 1/2 cup brewed coffee
- sweetener of your choice (optional)
- cinnamon powder (optional)

Instructions:

1- In a small saucepan, heat the soy milk over medium heat until it starts to steam. Do not let it boil.
2- While the milk is heating up, brew your espresso or coffee.
3- Once the milk is heated, pour it into a blender and blend on high for 15-20 seconds until it becomes frothy.
4- Pour the coffee into a large mug or cup.
5- Pour the frothy soy milk over the coffee, using a spoon to hold back the froth if necessary.
6- Spoon the froth on top of the coffee.
7- Add sweetener to taste if desired and stir.
8- Enjoy your delicious soy milk cappuccino coffee!

Chapter 4: Non-Dairy Coffee Recipes

RECIPE NO#33
COCONUT MILK

Ingredients:

- 1 cup coconut milk
- 1-2 shots of espresso or 1/2 cup brewed coffee
- 1 tablespoon unsweetened cocoa powder
- sweetener of your choice (optional)

Instructions:

1- In a small saucepan, heat the coconut milk over medium heat until it starts to steam. Do not let it boil.
2- While the milk is heating up, brew your espresso or coffee.
3- Once the milk is heated, add the cocoa powder and whisk until well combined.
4- Pour the coffee into a large mug or cup.
5- Pour the coconut milk and cocoa mixture over the coffee.
6- Add sweetener to taste if desired and stir.
7- Enjoy your delicious coconut milk mocha! Optional
8- toppings include whipped cream or a sprinkle of cinnamon.

Chapter 4: Non-Dairy Coffee Recipes

RECIPE NO#34
OAT MILK LATTE

Ingredients:

- 1 cup of oat milk
-- 1-2 shots of espresso (or strong brewed coffee)
- Sweetener of your choice (optional)

Instructions:

1. Heat up your oat milk in a saucepan over medium heat until it reaches your desired temperature. Do not boil the milk.
2. While the milk is heating, prepare your espresso or strong brewed coffee.
3. Once the milk is heated, froth it using a milk frother until it becomes nice and creamy.
4. Pour the frothed oat milk into a mug and add the espresso or coffee.
5. Sweeten the latte with your choice of sweetener, if desired.
6. Give the latte a good stir, and enjoy!

Chapter 4: Non-Dairy Coffee Recipes

RECIPE NO#35
HEMP MILK COFFEE

Ingredients:

- 1 cup freshly brewed coffee
- 1 cup unsweetened hemp milk
- 1-2 teaspoons honey or other sweetener (optional)
- 1/4 teaspoon vanilla extract (optional)

Instructions:

1. Start by brewing a cup of coffee using your preferred method.
2. In a small saucepan, heat the hemp milk over low to medium heat. Make sure not to boil it, as it may cause the milk to separate.
3. Once the hemp milk is warm, use a whisk to froth it until it becomes bubbly and frothy. You can also use a frother if you have one.
4. Pour the coffee into a mug, and add any sweeteners or vanilla extract you like.
5. Pour the frothed hemp milk over the coffee, using a spoon to hold back the foam until you have poured most of the milk. Then add the foam on top of the coffee.
6. Use a spoon or a skewer to create a latte art design on top of the foam, if desired.
7. Serve the hemp milk coffee immediately, and enjoy!

Chapter 4: Non-Dairy Coffee Recipes

RECIPE NO#36
CASHEW MILK

Ingredients:

- 1 cup cashew milk
- 1 shot of espresso or 1/4 cup of strong brewed coffee
- 1-2 teaspoons of honey (optional)
- Cinnamon powder or cocoa powder for garnish

Instructions:

1. Start by heating up the cashew milk in a small saucepan over medium heat until it is hot but not boiling.
2. While the milk is heating, brew the espresso or strong coffee.
3. Once the milk is hot, use a milk frother to froth the milk until it is foamy and has a silky texture. If you don't have a milk frother, you can pour the milk into a jar with a tight-fitting lid, and shake it vigorously until it becomes frothy.
4. Pour the espresso or coffee into a mug.
5. Add honey to the espresso or coffee (optional) and stir until the honey is dissolved.
6. Pour the frothy cashew milk over the espresso or coffee.
7. Garnish with a sprinkle of cinnamon powder or cocoa powder.
8. Serve hot and enjoy your delicious Cashew Milk Cappuccino!

Chapter 4: Non-Dairy Coffee Recipes

RECIPE NO#37
MACADAMIA NUT

Ingredients:

- 1 shot of espresso or 1/2 cup of strong coffee
- 1 cup of milk (dairy or non-dairy)
- 1 tablespoon of macadamia nut syrup
- Whipped cream (optional)
- Crushed macadamia nuts (optional)

Instructions:

1. Brew a shot of espresso or make 1/2 cup of strong coffee using your preferred method.
2. In a small saucepan, heat the milk over medium heat until hot, but not boiling. If using dairy milk, froth it using a milk frother or whisk until it becomes frothy and has a velvety texture.
3. Add the macadamia nut syrup to the hot coffee and stir until it's fully mixed in.
4. Pour the hot milk over the coffee and syrup mixture, spooning the frothed milk on top.
5. Top with whipped cream and sprinkle with crushed macadamia nuts, if desired.
6. Enjoy your delicious macadamia nut latte while it's still hot!

Chapter 4: Non-Dairy Coffee Recipes

RECIPE NO#38
PEA MILK MOCHA

Ingredients:

- 1 cup brewed coffee
- 1/2 cup unsweetened pea milk
- 1 tablespoon unsweetened cocoa powder
- 1 tablespoon maple syrup
- Optional toppings: whipped cream and cocoa powder

Instructions:

1. Brew your favorite coffee according to your preference.
2. In a small saucepan, heat the pea milk on medium heat until hot, but not boiling.
3. Whisk in the cocoa powder and maple syrup until well combined and smooth.
4. Pour the hot pea milk mixture into the brewed coffee and stir until well combined.
5. Optional: top with whipped cream and a sprinkle of cocoa powder.
6. Serve hot and enjoy!

Chapter 4: Non-Dairy Coffee Recipes

RECIPE NO#39
RICE MILK LATTE

Ingredients:

- 1 cup of cooked white rice
- 4 cups of water
- 2 tablespoons of honey or any other sweetener (optional)
- 1 teaspoon of vanilla extract (optional)
- 1 shot of espresso or 1/2 cup of strong brewed coffee
- 1/2 cup of rice milk

Instructions:

1. Rinse the cooked rice thoroughly under cold water and then drain it.
2. In a blender, add the cooked rice and 4 cups of water, and blend until the mixture is smooth and creamy.
3. Pour the mixture through a fine mesh sieve into a pot, and bring it to a simmer over medium heat.
4. Reduce the heat to low and let the mixture simmer for about 20-25 minutes, stirring occasionally to prevent it from sticking to the bottom of the pot.
5. Add the sweetener and vanilla extract (if using), and continue to simmer for another 5-10 minutes until the mixture thickens.
6. Remove the pot from the heat and let it cool slightly.
7. In a separate pot or saucepan, heat the rice milk over low heat until warm.
8. Add the rice milk to the rice mixture and stir well.
9. Pour the mixture through a fine mesh sieve into a large mug or two smaller ones.
10. Add a shot of espresso or 1/2 cup of strong brewed coffee to the mug(s), and stir well.
11. Serve immediately and enjoy your delicious Rice Milk Latte!

Chapter 4: Non-Dairy Coffee Recipes

RECIPE NO#40
SUNFLOWER SEED

Ingredients:

- 1/2 cup sunflower seeds
- 4 cups filtered water
- 1-2 tablespoons honey or sweetener of choice (optional)
- 1-2 shots of espresso or 1/2-1 cup of brewed coffee

Instructions:

1. Soak sunflower seeds in water overnight or for at least 6 hours. Drain and rinse the seeds thoroughly.
2. Add the soaked sunflower seeds and 4 cups of filtered water to a blender. Blend on high for 1-2 minutes or until the mixture is smooth and creamy.
3. Strain the sunflower seed milk through a nut milk bag or cheesecloth into a pitcher or large jar. Squeeze the bag or cheesecloth to extract as much milk as possible.
4. If desired, sweeten the sunflower seed milk with honey or your preferred sweetener.
5. Heat the sunflower seed milk on the stovetop or in the microwave until it's warm but not boiling.
6. Brew a shot or two of espresso, or prepare 1/2-1 cup of brewed coffee.
7. Pour the espresso or coffee into a mug, and then add the warm sunflower seed milk.
8. Stir to combine, and enjoy your Sunflower Seed Milk Coffee!

Chapter 5: Boozy Coffee Recipes

RECIPE NO#41
BAILEYS IRISH CREAM

Ingredients:

- 1 cup freshly brewed hot coffee
- 1 oz Baileys Irish Cream liqueur
- Whipped cream (optional)
- Chocolate shavings (optional)

Instructions:

1. Brew your coffee using your preferred method.
2. While the coffee is still hot, pour 1 oz of Baileys Irish Cream liqueur into your coffee mug.
3. Stir the coffee and Baileys together until well combined.
4. If desired, top with whipped cream and chocolate shavings for added indulgence.
5. Serve and enjoy your delicious Baileys Irish Cream Coffee!

Chapter 5: Boozy Coffee Recipes

RECIPE NO#42
KAHLUA COFFEE

Ingredients:

- 1 cup of strong coffee
- 1 oz Kahlua liqueur
- 1-2 teaspoons of sugar (optional)
- Whipped cream (optional)
- Chocolate shavings (optional)

Instructions:

1. Brew one cup of strong coffee using your preferred brewing method. It can be either drip, French press, or any other method you like.
2. Pour one ounce of Kahlua liqueur into the coffee and stir to combine.
3. Taste the coffee and add sugar if desired.
4. Top with whipped cream and chocolate shavings if desired.
5. Serve and enjoy your delicious Kahlua coffee!

Chapter 5: Boozy Coffee Recipes

RECIPE NO#43
BRANDY ALEXANDER

Ingredients:

- 1 cup of hot coffee
- 1/4 cup of brandy
- 1/4 cup of crème de cacao liqueur
- 1/2 cup of heavy cream
- 1 teaspoon of granulated sugar
- Freshly grated nutmeg for garnish

Instructions:

1. Brew a cup of coffee and set aside.
2. In a mixing glass, combine the brandy and crème de cacao liqueur.
3. Fill a cocktail shaker with ice, and pour the brandy and liqueur mixture over the ice.
4. Shake the cocktail shaker vigorously for about 10-15 seconds to chill the mixture.
5. Strain the brandy and liqueur mixture into a heat-resistant glass.
6. Pour the hot coffee into the glass with the brandy and liqueur mixture.
7. In a separate mixing bowl, whisk together the heavy cream and sugar until stiff peaks form.
8. Spoon the whipped cream over the top of the coffee and liqueur mixture in the glass.
9. Garnish with freshly grated nutmeg.
10. Serve immediately and enjoy your delicious Brandy Alexander Coffee!

Chapter 5: Boozy Coffee Recipes

RECIPE NO#44
IRISH COFFEE

Ingredients:

- 2 oz Irish whiskey
- 1 oz Kahlua
- 1 oz strong coffee, chilled
- 1 oz heavy cream
- 1/2 oz simple syrup + Ice
- Ground cinnamon, for garnish

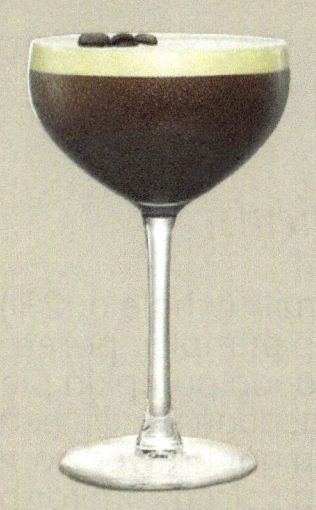

Instructions:

1. Begin by chilling a martini glass in the freezer for 5-10 minutes.
2. In a cocktail shaker, combine the Irish whiskey, Kahlua, chilled coffee, heavy cream, and simple syrup.
3. Fill the shaker with ice, and shake vigorously for about 15 seconds, until the ingredients are well combined and the mixture is chilled.
4. Strain the mixture into the chilled martini glass.
5. Dust the top of the cocktail with a sprinkle of ground cinnamon for a fragrant and visually appealing garnish.
6. Serve your Irish Coffee Martini immediately, and enjoy!

Chapter 5: Boozy Coffee Recipes

RECIPE NO#45
SPIKED PUMPKIN

Ingredients:

- 1 cup milk (whole or 2%)
- 1/2 cup pumpkin puree + 2 tablespoons brown sugar
- 1 teaspoon pumpkin pie spice
- 1/2 teaspoon vanilla extract
- 1/2 cup hot brewed coffee
- 1/2 cup spiced rum (or bourbon)

Instructions:

1. In a small saucepan over medium heat, whisk together the milk, pumpkin puree, brown sugar, pumpkin pie spice, and vanilla extract. Continue whisking until the mixture is heated through and well combined.
2. In a separate mug, brew your coffee.
3. Once the pumpkin milk mixture is heated, remove it from the heat and stir in the spiced rum (or bourbon).
4. Pour the pumpkin spice mixture over the brewed coffee and stir to combine.
5. If desired, top with whipped cream and a sprinkle of cinnamon.

Chapter 5: Boozy Coffee Recipes

RECIPE NO#46
WHISKEY COFFEE

Ingredients:

- 1 cup of hot brewed coffee
- 1 shot of whiskey (about 1.5 oz)
- 1 tablespoon of brown sugar
- 1 tablespoon of heavy cream-
- Whipped cream (optional)
- Cinnamon (optional)

Instructions:

1. Brew your favorite coffee and pour it into a mug.
2. Add a shot of whiskey to the coffee and stir.
3. Stir in the brown sugar until it has completely dissolved.
4. Add the heavy cream to the coffee and stir gently.
5. Optional: Top with whipped cream and sprinkle with cinnamon.
6. Enjoy your delicious Whiskey Coffee!

Chapter 5: Boozy Coffee Recipes

RECIPE NO#48
CHOCOLATE RASPBERRY MARTINI

Ingredients:

- 2 oz chocolate vodka
- 1 oz raspberry liqueur
- 1 oz chilled espresso
- 1 oz half-and-half
- Ice cubes
- Chocolate syrup and fresh raspberries, for garnish

Instructions:

1. Chill a martini glass in the freezer for at least 10 minutes.
2. Fill a cocktail shaker with ice.
3. Add the chocolate vodka, raspberry liqueur, chilled espresso, and half-and-half to the shaker.
4. Shake vigorously for about 15 seconds.
5. Drizzle chocolate syrup inside the chilled martini glass.
6. Strain the cocktail from the shaker into the prepared martini glass.
7. Garnish with a few fresh raspberries on a cocktail pick.
8. Serve and enjoy your delicious Chocolate Raspberry Martini Coffee!

Chapter 5: Boozy Coffee Recipes

RECIPE NO#49
VANILLA VODKA

Ingredients:

- 1 shot of espresso
- 1 1/2 oz of vanilla vodka
- 1 cup of milk
- 1 tbsp of vanilla syrup
- Whipped cream (optional)
- Ground cinnamon (optional)

Instructions:

1. Brew a shot of espresso and set it aside.
2. In a small saucepan, heat up the milk on low heat until it is warm but not boiling.
3. Once the milk is warm, add the vanilla syrup and stir until it is fully mixed in.
4. In a separate mug, pour in the vanilla vodka and the shot of espresso.
5. Pour the warm vanilla milk into the mug and stir everything together.
6. Top with whipped cream and a sprinkle of ground cinnamon (optional).
7. Serve and enjoy your delicious Vanilla Vodka Latte!

Chapter 5: Boozy Coffee Recipes

RECIPE NO#50
BOURBON CARAMEL

Ingredients:

- 2 shots of espresso
- 1 cup of milk
- 1 tablespoon of caramel sauce
- 1 tablespoon of bourbon
- Whipped cream (optional)
- Caramel drizzle (optional)

Instructions:

1. Start by brewing two shots of espresso and set it aside.
2. In a saucepan, heat the milk over medium heat until it starts to steam.
3. Add the caramel sauce and bourbon to the saucepan and stir until well combined.
4. Use a milk frother to froth the milk mixture until it's nice and creamy.
5. Pour the frothed milk mixture into a mug.
6. Add the two shots of espresso to the mug and stir gently.
7. Top with whipped cream and a drizzle of caramel sauce, if desired.
8. Serve immediately and enjoy your delicious Bourbon Caramel Latte!

Chapter 6: Unique Coffee Recipes

RECIPE NO#51
COFFEE COLADA

Ingredients:

- 1 cup strong coffee, cooled
- 1/2 cup coconut milk
- 1/4 cup pineapple juice
- 1 tablespoon honey or maple syrup
- 1 cup ice
- Optional: whipped cream and coconut flakes for topping

Instructions:

1. Brew a cup of strong coffee and let it cool to room temperature or chill in the refrigerator.
2. In a blender, add the cooled coffee, coconut milk, pineapple juice, honey or maple syrup, and ice.
3. Blend the ingredients until smooth and frothy.
4. Pour the coffee colada into a glass and top with whipped cream and coconut flakes if desired.
5. Serve and enjoy your refreshing and tropical coffee colada!

Chapter 6: Unique Coffee Recipes

RECIPE NO#52
COFFEE SANGRIA

Ingredients:

- 2 cups brewed strong coffee, cooled
- 1 cup red wine + 1/2 cup brandy
- 1/4 cup honey + 1 orange, sliced
- 1 lemon, sliced + 1 lime, sliced
- 1 cinnamon stick + 1/4 teaspoon nutmeg
- 1/4 teaspoon cloves + Ice cubes + Sparkling water

Instructions:

1. In a large pitcher, combine the cooled coffee, red wine, brandy, and honey. Stir well until the honey is fully dissolved.
2. Add the sliced orange, lemon, and lime to the pitcher. Add the cinnamon stick, nutmeg, and cloves.
3. Stir everything together and refrigerate for at least 2 hours (or overnight) to allow the flavors to meld together.
4. When ready to serve, fill glasses with ice cubes. Pour the coffee sangria over the ice, leaving some space at the top of each glass.
5. Top each glass with sparkling water or club soda, to taste.
6. Garnish with fresh mint leaves, if desired, and serve immediately.

Chapter 6: Unique Coffee Recipes

RECIPE NO#53
COFFEE SMOOTHIE

Ingredients:

- 1 cup brewed coffee, chilled
- 1 banana, sliced-
- 1/2 cup plain Greek yogurt
- 1/4 cup almond milk
- 1 tablespoon honey + 1/2 teaspoon vanilla extract
- 1/2 cup ice cubes

Instructions:

1. Brew 1 cup of coffee and let it cool. You can also use leftover coffee from the morning and chill it in the fridge.
2. In a blender, add the cooled coffee, sliced banana, Greek yogurt, almond milk, honey, and vanilla extract.
3. Blend the ingredients until they are smooth and well combined.
4. Add the ice cubes and blend again until the smoothie is thick and frothy.
5. Pour the coffee smoothie into a glass and serve immediately. You can also add whipped cream or chocolate shavings on top for an extra indulgent treat.

Chapter 6: Unique Coffee Recipes

RECIPE NO#54
COFFEE MILKSHAKE

Ingredients:

- 1 cup brewed coffee, chilled
- 2 cups vanilla ice cream
- 1/2 cup milk
- 1 tbsp sugar
- Whipped cream, for topping (optional)

Instructions:

1. Brew a cup of coffee and let it cool down completely. You can also use leftover coffee from the morning and chill it in the fridge.
2. In a blender, add the chilled coffee, vanilla ice cream, milk, and sugar. Blend the ingredients until smooth.
3. If the mixture is too thick, add more milk until it reaches your desired consistency.
4. Pour the coffee milkshake into a tall glass.
5. Add a dollop of whipped cream on top, if desired.
6. Serve immediately and enjoy your delicious coffee milkshake!

Chapter 6: Unique Coffee Recipes

Recipe No#55
Chocolate Covered Cherry Coffee

Ingredients:

- 1 cup brewed coffee
- 1/4 cup cherry syrup
- 1/4 cup chocolate syrup
- 1/4 cup milk or cream
- Whipped cream and chocolate shavings for topping

Instructions:

1. Brew a cup of coffee using your preferred method and pour it into a large mug.
2. Add the cherry syrup and chocolate syrup to the coffee and stir until well combined.
3. Warm the milk or cream in a small saucepan over low heat or in the microwave until hot.
4. Pour the warm milk or cream into the coffee mixture and stir.
5. If desired, top with whipped cream and chocolate shavings.
6. Enjoy your delicious Chocolate Covered Cherry Coffee!

Chapter 6: Unique Coffee Recipes

RECIPE NO#56
COFFEE JULEP

Ingredients:

- 1 1/2 oz coffee liqueur
- 1 oz bourbon whiskey
- 1/2 oz simple syrup
- 8-10 fresh mint leaves
- Crushed ice
- Mint sprigs for garnish

Instructions:

1. In a cocktail shaker, muddle the fresh mint leaves with the simple syrup until the leaves are bruised and fragrant.
2. Add the coffee liqueur and bourbon whiskey to the shaker, and fill it with ice.
3. Shake well until the mixture is thoroughly combined and chilled.
4. Fill a julep cup or glass with crushed ice.
5. Strain the cocktail into the glass, over the ice.
6. Garnish with a sprig of fresh mint.

Chapter 6: Unique Coffee Recipes

RECIPE NO#57
BLUEBERRY COFFEE

Ingredients:

- 1 cup fresh blueberries
- 1/4 cup sugar + 1/4 cup water
- 1 cup freshly brewed coffee
- 1/4 cup milk (or dairy-free alternative)
- Whipped cream (optional)
- Fresh blueberries for garnish (optional)

Instructions:

1. In a small saucepan, combine the fresh blueberries, sugar, and water. Bring to a simmer over medium heat, stirring occasionally, until the blueberries have broken down and the mixture has thickened to a syrupy consistency, about 10 minutes.
2. Remove the blueberry syrup from heat and let it cool for a few minutes.
3. In a coffee mug, pour the freshly brewed coffee.
4. Add the milk to the coffee and stir to combine.
5. Pour the blueberry syrup over the coffee and milk mixture and stir gently.
6. Top with whipped cream and fresh blueberries, if desired.

Chapter 6: Unique Coffee Recipes

RECIPE NO#58
COFFEE MARGARITA

Ingredients:

-- 2 oz tequila
- 1 oz Kahlua or coffee liqueur
- 1 oz fresh lime juice + 1 oz simple syrup
- 1/2 oz triple sec + 1/2 cup of ice
- Coarse salt, for rimming glass
- Lime wedge, for garnish

Instructions:

1. Rim a chilled margarita glass with coarse salt. To do this, rub the rim of the glass with a lime wedge, then dip the rim into a small dish of coarse salt, rotating the glass to coat the rim evenly. Set the glass aside.
2. In a shaker, combine the tequila, Kahlua or coffee liqueur, fresh lime juice, simple syrup, triple sec, and ice.
3. Shake vigorously for about 15-20 seconds until well chilled.
4. Strain the mixture into the prepared glass.
5. Garnish with a lime wedge.
6. Enjoy your coffee margarita!

Chapter 6: Unique Coffee Recipes

RECIPE NO#59
LEMON COFFEE

Ingredients:

- 2 cups of freshly brewed coffee
- 1/2 cup of fresh lemon juice
- 1/4 cup of honey
- 1 teaspoon of vanilla extract
- Lemon slices, for garnish

Instructions:

1. Begin by brewing 2 cups of your favorite coffee.
2. In a separate bowl, mix together 1/2 cup of fresh lemon juice, 1/4 cup of honey, and 1 teaspoon of vanilla extract.
3. Once the coffee is finished brewing, pour it into a large mixing bowl. Then, add the lemon-honey-vanilla mixture and whisk everything together until well combined.
4. Pour the Lemon Coffee into serving mugs and garnish with a slice of lemon.
5. Serve hot and enjoy!

Chapter 6: Unique Coffee Recipes

RECIPE NO#60
LAVENDER HONEY

Ingredients:

- 1 shot of espresso (or 1/2 cup strong brewed coffee)
- 1/2 cup milk
- 1 tablespoon honey
- 1/4 teaspoon dried lavender
- Whipped cream (optional)

Instructions:

1. Brew one shot of espresso or make 1/2 cup of strong brewed coffee.
2. In a small saucepan, heat milk, honey, and dried lavender over medium heat. Whisk occasionally until the milk is steaming and the honey is melted.
3. Remove the pan from the heat and let it sit for a few minutes to allow the lavender to infuse into the milk.
4. Strain the milk mixture through a fine-mesh sieve to remove the lavender.
5. Froth the milk mixture using a milk frother, or by vigorously shaking the mixture in a jar with a tight-fitting lid until it becomes frothy.
6. Pour the frothed milk into the espresso or coffee and stir to combine.
7. Top with whipped cream if desired and a sprinkle of dried lavender on top.

Chapter 7: International Coffee

RECIPE NO#61
TURKISH COFFEE

Ingredients:

- 1 cup cold water
- 2 tablespoons Turkish coffee grounds (finely ground)
- Sugar (optional)

Instructions:

1. Measure out 1 cup of cold water into a small pot called a cezve. Place it over medium heat on the stove.
2. Add 2 tablespoons of finely ground Turkish coffee to the cezve. If you prefer your coffee sweet, you can also add sugar to taste at this point.
3. Using a small spoon, stir the coffee grounds and water until they are well combined.
4. Continue to heat the coffee over medium heat, stirring occasionally, until it comes to a boil. Be sure to keep a close eye on the coffee to prevent it from boiling over.
5. Once the coffee starts to boil and foam up, remove the cezve from the heat and let it sit for a few seconds to allow the foam to settle.
6. Return the cezve to the heat and allow it to boil and foam up again. Repeat this process one or two more times until the coffee has a thick, frothy texture.
7. Once the coffee is ready, pour it into small coffee cups and serve immediately. Be sure to serve with a small glass of water, as it is customary to drink water before and after drinking Turkish coffee.

Chapter 7: International Coffee

RECIPE NO#62
GREEK FRAPPE

Ingredients:

- 2 tsp instant coffee
- 2 tsp granulated sugar
- 2-3 ice cubes
- 1/4 cup cold water
- Milk (optional)

Instructions:

1. In a tall glass or cocktail shaker, add the instant coffee and granulated sugar.
2. Add about 1/4 cup of cold water to the glass or shaker. You can adjust the amount of water depending on how strong you like your coffee.
3. Use a handheld frother or a cocktail shaker with a tight lid to mix the coffee, sugar, and water together until they form a frothy mixture. This should take about 30 seconds to a minute.
4. Fill the glass with 2-3 ice cubes.
5. Pour the frothy coffee mixture over the ice cubes in the glass.
6. If desired, top up the glass with cold milk.
7. Stir the coffee with a long spoon to combine the milk and coffee (if using).
8. Serve and enjoy your delicious Greek frappe coffee!

Chapter 7: International Coffee

RECIPE NO#63
ITALIAN BICERIN

Ingredients:

- 1 shot espresso
- 1/3 cup whole milk
- 1/3 cup hot chocolate or chocolate syrup
- Whipped cream (optional)
- Shaved chocolate (optional)

Instructions:

1. Make a shot of espresso and pour it into a small glass or cup.
2. In a separate saucepan, heat up the whole milk until it's hot but not boiling.
3. Pour the hot milk into the glass or cup with the espresso.
4. In another small saucepan, heat up the hot chocolate or chocolate syrup until it's warm.
5. Pour the warm chocolate on top of the milk and espresso mixture in the glass or cup.
6. If desired, top with whipped cream and shaved chocolate.
7. Serve and enjoy your delicious Italian Bicerin!

Chapter 7: International Coffee

RECIPE NO#64
SPANISH CAFE CON

Ingredients:

- 1 shot of espresso
- 1/2 cup whole milk
- 1-2 tsp sugar (optional)

Instructions:

1. Make a shot of espresso and pour it into a small saucepan.
2. Heat up the espresso on medium heat.
3. Add the whole milk to the saucepan and heat it up together with the espresso.
4. Stir the mixture constantly until it starts to steam and the milk is heated through.
5. Remove the saucepan from heat.
6. If desired, add 1-2 teaspoons of sugar to the mixture and stir until the sugar is dissolved.
7. Pour the mixture into a coffee cup or mug.
8. Serve and enjoy your delicious Spanish Cafe con Leche!

Chapter 7: International Coffee

RECIPE NO#65
FRENCH CAFE AU LAIT

Ingredients:

- 1 cup freshly brewed coffee
- 1 cup whole milk
- 1-2 tsp sugar (optional)

Instructions:

1. Brew a cup of coffee using your preferred brewing method.
2. In a small saucepan, heat up the whole milk on medium heat until it starts to steam and is heated through.
3. Pour the coffee into a coffee mug or bowl.
4. If desired, add 1-2 teaspoons of sugar to the coffee and stir until the sugar is dissolved.
5. Pour the heated milk into the coffee mug or bowl, making sure to leave some room at the top for froth.
6. Using a frother or a blender, froth the milk until it becomes light and frothy.
7. Spoon the frothy milk on top of the coffee.
8. Serve and enjoy your delicious French Cafe au Lait!

Chapter 7: International Coffee

RECIPE NO#66
MOROCCAN SPICED

Ingredients:

- 1 cup strong brewed coffee
- 1/4 tsp ground cinnamon
- 1/8 tsp ground cardamom
- 1/8 tsp ground nutmeg
- 1/8 tsp ground ginger
- 1 tbsp honey

Instructions:

1. Brew a cup of strong coffee using your preferred brewing method.
2. In a small bowl, mix together the ground cinnamon, cardamom, nutmeg, and ginger.
3. Add the spice mixture to the coffee and stir well.
4. Add honey to the coffee and stir until it's fully dissolved.
5. In a separate saucepan, heat up the milk on medium heat until it's hot but not boiling.
6. If desired, froth the milk using a frother or a blender.
7. Pour the hot or frothed milk into the spiced coffee.
8. If desired, top with whipped cream and a sprinkle of cinnamon.
9. Serve and enjoy your delicious Moroccan Spiced Coffee!

Chapter 7: International Coffee

RECIPE NO#67
VIETNAMESSE EGG

Ingredients:

- 2 tbsp condensed milk
- 2 tbsp hot water
- 1 egg
- 1 cup hot brewed coffee
- Ground cinnamon (optional)

Instructions:

1. In a small bowl, whisk together the condensed milk and hot water until it's fully dissolved.
2. In a separate bowl, whisk the egg until it's frothy and pale in color.
3. Add the condensed milk mixture to the bowl with the egg and whisk until it's well combined.
4. Brew a cup of hot coffee using your preferred brewing method.
5. Pour the egg mixture into a coffee mug.
6. Pour the hot coffee into the mug, slowly pouring it over the egg mixture.
7. Stir the coffee and egg mixture together until it's well combined.
8. If desired, sprinkle some ground cinnamon on top for added flavor.
9. Serve and enjoy your delicious Vietnamese Egg Coffee!

Chapter 7: International Coffee

RECIPE No#68
ETHIOPIAN COFFEE

Ingredients:

- 1 cup freshly roasted Ethiopian coffee beans
Water
- Jebena (traditional Ethiopian coffee pot)
- Charcoal or wood for roasting
- Small dishes for serving coffee and snacks (optional)

Instructions:

1. In a small bowl, whisk together the condensed milk and hot water until it's fully dissolved.
2. In a separate bowl, whisk the egg until it's frothy and pale in color.
3. Add the condensed milk mixture to the bowl with the egg and whisk until it's well combined.
4. Brew a cup of hot coffee using your preferred brewing method.
5. Pour the egg mixture into a coffee mug.
6. Pour the hot coffee into the mug, slowly pouring it over the egg mixture.
7. Stir the coffee and egg mixture together until it's well combined.
8. If desired, sprinkle some ground cinnamon on top for added flavor.
9. Serve and enjoy your delicious Vietnamese Egg Coffee!

Chapter 7: International Coffee

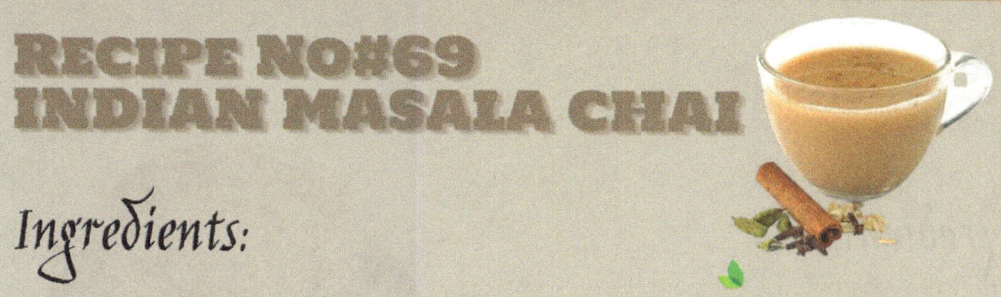

RECIPE NO#69
INDIAN MASALA CHAI

Ingredients:

- 2 cups water
- 2 black tea bags or tbsp loose black tea leaves
- 1 cinnamon stick + 4-5 whole cloves
- 4-5 cardamom pods
- 1 piece of fresh ginger, peeled and sliced
- 1 cup milk + 2-3 tbsp sugar or honey (optional)

Instructions:

1. In a medium-sized pot, add water, cinnamon stick, cloves, cardamom pods, and fresh ginger. Bring the mixture to a boil.
2. Reduce the heat to low and let the spices and ginger simmer for 5-10 minutes to infuse the water with their flavors.
3. Add the black tea bags or loose tea leaves to the pot and let them steep for 3-5 minutes.
4. Add the milk and sugar or honey to the pot and stir well.
5. Increase the heat to medium and bring the mixture to a simmer.
6. Once the chai has simmered for a few minutes, remove it from the heat.
7. Strain the chai using a fine-mesh strainer into a teapot or individual cups.
8. Serve the chai hot and enjoy your delicious Indian Masala Chai!

Chapter 7: International Coffee

RECIPE NO#70
MEXICAN CAFE OLLA

Ingredients:

- 4 cups water
- 2-3 cinnamon sticks
- 1/4 cup piloncillo or brown sugar
- 4-5 whole cloves
- 2 tbsp coarsely ground coffee

Instructions:

1. In a medium-sized pot, add water, cinnamon sticks, piloncillo or brown sugar, and cloves. Bring the mixture to a boil.
2. Reduce the heat to low and let the mixture simmer for 5-10 minutes to infuse the water with the flavors.
3. Add the coarsely ground coffee to the pot and stir well.
4. Increase the heat to medium and bring the mixture to a simmer.
5. Once the coffee has brewed for a few minutes, remove it from the heat.
6. Let the mixture rest for 5-10 minutes to allow the coffee grounds to settle to the bottom of the pot.
7. Pour the coffee through a fine-mesh strainer into a mug or pitcher.
8. Serve the Cafe de Olla hot and enjoy your delicious Mexican coffee!

Chapter 8: Keto Coffee Recipes

RECIPE NO#71
MCT OIL COFFEE

Ingredients:

- 1 cup freshly brewed coffee
- 1 tbsp grass-fed butter or ghee
- 1 tbsp MCT oil or coconut oil

Instructions:

1. Brew 1 cup of coffee using your preferred method.
2. While the coffee is still hot, pour it into a blender along with grass-fed butter or ghee and MCT oil or coconut oil.
3. Blend on high speed for 20-30 seconds until the mixture is frothy and well combined.
4. Pour the Bulletproof Coffee into a mug and enjoy your delicious and creamy coffee!

Chapter 8: Keto Coffee Recipes

RECIPE NO#72
BUTTER COFFEE

Ingredients:

- 1 cup freshly brewed coffee
- 1 tbsp unsalted grass-fed butter
- 1 tbsp coconut oil or MCT oil (optional)

Instructions:

1. Brew 1 cup of coffee using your preferred method.
2. While the coffee is still hot, add unsalted grass-fed butter to the cup.
3. If using, add coconut oil or MCT oil to the cup as well.
4. Using a blender, blend the coffee, butter, and optional coconut oil or MCT oil on high speed for 20-30 seconds until the mixture is frothy and well combined.
5. Pour the Butter Coffee back into the cup and enjoy your creamy and delicious coffee!

Chapter 8: Keto Coffee Recipes

RECIPE NO#73
COCONUT OIL COFFEE

Ingredients:

- 1 cup freshly brewed coffee
- 1-2 tbsp virgin coconut oil
- Optional: sweetener, such as honey or maple syrup

Instructions:

1. Brew 1 cup of coffee using your preferred method.
2. While the coffee is still hot, add 1-2 tbsp of virgin coconut oil to the cup.
3. Stir the coffee and coconut oil until the oil is fully melted and blended into the coffee.
4. If desired, add a sweetener such as honey or maple syrup and stir until dissolved.
5. Enjoy your delicious and creamy Coconut Oil Coffee!

Chapter 8: Keto Coffee Recipes

RECIPE NO#74
TURMERIC COFFEE

Ingredients:

- 1 cup freshly brewed coffee
- 1 tsp ground turmeric
- 1/2 tsp ground cinnamon
- 1/2 tsp ground ginger
- 1 tsp honey (optional)
- 1/2 cup almond milk or any other milk of your choice

Instructions:

1. Brew 1 cup of coffee using your preferred method.
2. In a small bowl, mix together ground turmeric, ground cinnamon, and ground ginger.
3. Pour the brewed coffee into a saucepan and heat it on low heat.
4. Add the spice mixture to the coffee and whisk until well combined.
5. If desired, add honey and stir until dissolved.
6. Add almond milk or any other milk of your choice to the coffee mixture and whisk until frothy and well combined.
7. Pour the Turmeric Coffee into a mug and enjoy your delicious and healthy coffee!

Chapter 8: Keto Coffee Recipes

RECIPE NO#75
CINNAMON COFFEE

Ingredients:

- 1 cup freshly brewed coffee
- 1/2 tsp ground cinnamon
- 1 tsp honey (optional)
- 1/4 cup milk of your choice (optional)

Instructions:

1. Brew 1 cup of coffee using your preferred method.
2. In a small bowl, mix together ground cinnamon and honey.
3. Pour the brewed coffee into a mug.
4. Add the cinnamon and honey mixture to the coffee and stir until well combined.
5. If desired, heat up milk of your choice in a small saucepan and froth using a frother or whisk until it reaches your desired consistency.
6. Pour the milk into the coffee and stir until well combined.
7. Enjoy your delicious and aromatic Cinnamon Coffee!

Chapter 8: Keto Coffee Recipes

Recipe No#76
Matcha Latee with Coconut Oil

Ingredients:

- 1 tsp matcha powder
- 1 tsp honey (optional)
- 1 tsp virgin coconut oil
- 1/2 cup hot water
- 1/2 cup milk of your choice

Instructions:

1. In a small bowl, whisk together matcha powder and hot water until there are no clumps.
2. Add honey and virgin coconut oil to the bowl and whisk until well combined.
3. Heat up milk of your choice in a small saucepan and froth using a frother or whisk until it reaches your desired consistency.
4. Pour the matcha mixture into a mug.
5. Add frothed milk to the matcha mixture and stir until well combined.
6. Enjoy your delicious and healthy Matcha Latte with Coconut Oil!

Chapter 8: Keto Coffee Recipes

RECIPE NO#78
KETO MOCHA

Ingredients:

- 1 cup freshly brewed coffee
- 1 tbsp unsweetened cocoa powder
- 1 tbsp coconut oil
- 1 tsp vanilla extract
- 1/2 cup unsweetened almond milk

Instructions:

1. Brew 1 cup of coffee using your preferred method.
2. In a small saucepan, heat the almond milk on low heat until it's warm, but not boiling.
3. Add unsweetened cocoa powder, coconut oil, vanilla extract, and keto-friendly sweetener to the saucepan and whisk until well combined.
4. Use a frother or whisk to froth the almond milk mixture until it reaches your desired consistency.
5. Pour the brewed coffee into a mug.
6. Add the frothed almond milk mixture to the coffee and stir until well combined.
7. Enjoy your delicious and creamy Keto Mocha!

Chapter 8: Keto Coffee Recipes

RECIPE NO#79
COCOA BUTTER

Ingredients:

- 1 cup freshly brewed coffee
- 1 tbsp cocoa butter
- 1 tbsp coconut oil
- 1 tsp vanilla extract (optional)
- 1-2 tbsp sweetener

Instructions:

1. Brew 1 cup of coffee using your preferred method.
2. In a small saucepan, melt the cocoa butter and coconut oil over low heat.
3. Once the cocoa butter and coconut oil are melted, remove the saucepan from the heat and add in the vanilla extract and sweetener (if using).
4. Use a frother or whisk to froth the cocoa butter mixture until it becomes creamy and frothy.
5. Pour the brewed coffee into a mug.
6. Add the frothed cocoa butter mixture to the coffee and stir until well combined.
7. Enjoy your delicious and creamy Cocoa Butter Coffee!

Chapter 8: Keto Coffee Recipes

RECIPE NO#80
SPICED KETO

Ingredients:

- 1 cup freshly brewed coffee
- 1 tbsp coconut oil
- 1 tsp ground cinnamon
- 1/4 tsp ground nutmeg
- 1/4 tsp ground ginger
- 1/4 tsp ground cloves

Instructions:

1. Brew 1 cup of coffee using your preferred method.
2. In a small saucepan, heat the heavy cream on low heat until it's warm, but not boiling.
3. Add coconut oil, ground cinnamon, ground nutmeg, ground ginger, ground cloves, and keto-friendly sweetener to the saucepan and whisk until well combined.
4. Use a frother or whisk to froth the spiced cream mixture until it reaches your desired consistency.
5. Pour the brewed coffee into a mug.
6. Add the frothed spiced cream mixture to the coffee and stir until well combined.
7. Enjoy your delicious and spiced Keto Coffee!

Chapter 9: Gourmet Coffee Recipes

RECIPE NO#81
MAPLE BACON

Ingredients:

- 1 shot espresso or 1/2 cup strong brewed coffee
- 1/2 cup milk
- 2 tbsp maple syrup
- 1/4 tsp liquid smoke (optional)
- 1/2 tsp vanilla extract
- 2 strips of cooked bacon

Instructions:

1. Cook 2 strips of bacon until crispy, then chop them into small pieces and set them aside.
2. In a small saucepan, heat the milk, maple syrup, and liquid smoke (if using) over medium heat until warm.
3. Add the chopped bacon to the milk mixture and stir until well combined.
4. Brew a shot of espresso or prepare 1/2 cup of strong brewed coffee.
5. Pour the espresso or coffee into a mug.
6. Add the vanilla extract to the warm milk mixture and stir until well combined.
7. Use a frother or whisk to froth the milk mixture until it becomes creamy and frothy.
8. Pour the frothed milk mixture into the mug with the coffee.
9. Top with whipped cream (if desired) and sprinkle with chopped bacon.
10. Enjoy your delicious and savory Maple Bacon Latte!

Chapter 9: Gourmet Coffee Recipes

RECIPE NO#82
BLACK FOREST

Ingredients:

- 1 cup brewed coffee
- 1/2 cup milk + 2 tablespoons unsweetened cocoa powder
- 2 tablespoons cherry syrup
- 1 tablespoon sugar + Whipped cream, for topping
- Chocolate shavings, for topping
- Maraschino cherry, for garnish

Instructions:

1. Brew one cup of coffee using your preferred brewing method.
2. In a small saucepan, heat the milk over medium-low heat until steaming.
3. In a separate bowl, whisk together the cocoa powder, cherry syrup, and sugar until well combined.
4. Pour the cocoa mixture into the hot milk, whisking constantly, until fully combined.
5. Pour the coffee into a mug, then pour the cocoa-cherry milk mixture on top.
6. Top with a dollop of whipped cream, chocolate shavings, and a maraschino cherry.
7. Enjoy your delicious Black Forest Mocha Coffee!

Chapter 9: Gourmet Coffee Recipes

Recipe No#83
White Chocolate Raspberry Mocha

Ingredients:

- 1 cup brewed coffee + 1/2 cup milk
- 2 tablespoons white chocolate chips
- 2 tablespoons raspberry syrup
- Whipped cream, for topping
- Fresh raspberries, for topping
- White chocolate shavings, for topping

Instructions:

1. Brew one cup of coffee using your preferred brewing method.
2. In a small saucepan, heat the milk over medium-low heat until steaming.
3. Add the white chocolate chips to the milk and stir until fully melted.
4. Stir in the raspberry syrup until fully combined.
5. Pour the coffee into a mug, then pour the white chocolate raspberry milk mixture on top.
6. Top with a dollop of whipped cream, fresh raspberries, and white chocolate shavings.
7. Enjoy your delicious White Chocolate Raspberry Mocha!

Chapter 9: Gourmet Coffee Recipes

RECIPE NO#84
LAVENDER MOCHA

Ingredients:

- 1 cup brewed coffee + 1/2 cup milk
- 1 tablespoon dried culinary lavender
- 2 tablespoons dark chocolate chips
- 1 tablespoon sugar
- Whipped cream, for topping
- Lavender buds or fresh mint, for topping (optional)

Instructions:

1. Brew one cup of coffee using your preferred brewing method.
2. In a small saucepan, heat the milk over medium-low heat until steaming.
3. Add the dried lavender to the milk and let steep for about 5 minutes.
4. Strain the lavender out of the milk and return the milk to the saucepan.
5. Add the dark chocolate chips and sugar to the milk, stirring constantly, until fully melted and combined.
6. Pour the coffee into a mug, then pour the lavender chocolate milk mixture on top.
7. Top with a dollop of whipped cream and lavender buds or fresh mint, if desired.
8. Enjoy your delicious Lavender Mocha!

Chapter 9: Gourmet Coffee Recipes

RECIPE No#85
CARDAMOM LATTE

Ingredients:

- 1 cup brewed coffee or espresso
- 1/2 cup milk
- 1/4 teaspoon ground cardamom
- 1 tablespoon honey or sugar
- Whipped cream, for topping (optional)
- Ground cinnamon or cardamom, for topping (optional)

Instructions:

1. Brew one cup of coffee or espresso using your preferred brewing method.
2. In a small saucepan, heat the milk over medium-low heat until steaming.
3. Add the ground cardamom and honey or sugar to the milk, stirring constantly, until fully combined.
4. Pour the coffee or espresso into a mug, then pour the cardamom milk mixture on top.
5. Top with a dollop of whipped cream and a sprinkle of ground cinnamon or cardamom, if desired.
6. Enjoy your delicious Cardamom Latte!

Chapter 9: Gourmet Coffee Recipes

RECIPE NO#86
ROSEWATER LATTE

Ingredients:

- 1 cup of milk (dairy or non-dairy)
- 1 teaspoon of rosewater
- 1 shot of espresso or 1/2 cup of strong brewed coffee
- Sweetener of your choice (optional)
- Dried rose petals (optional, for garnish)

Instructions:

1. In a small saucepan, heat the milk over medium-low heat until it starts to steam.
2. Add the rosewater to the milk and whisk until well combined.
3. Brew a shot of espresso or make strong brewed coffee.
4. If desired, sweeten the milk with your preferred sweetener.
5. Pour the espresso or coffee into a large mug.
6. Slowly pour the milk and rosewater mixture over the espresso or coffee, holding back the foam with a spoon.
7. Spoon the foam on top of the latte.
8. Garnish with dried rose petals (if using).
9. Serve and enjoy your delicious rosewater latte!

Chapter 9: Gourmet Coffee Recipes

RECIPE NO#87
HONEY LAVENDER

Ingredients:

- 1 cup of milk (dairy or non-dairy)
- 1 tablespoon of dried lavender buds
- 1 tablespoon of honey
- 1 shot of espresso or 1/2 cup of strong brewed coffee
- Lavender sprigs (optional, for garnish)

Instructions:

1. In a small saucepan, heat the milk over medium-low heat until it starts to steam.
2. Add the dried lavender buds to the milk and whisk until well combined.
3. Brew a shot of espresso or make strong brewed coffee.
4. Add the honey to the espresso or coffee and stir until dissolved.
5. Slowly pour the lavender-infused milk over the espresso or coffee, holding back the foam with a spoon.
6. Spoon the foam on top of the latte.
7. Garnish with a sprig of lavender (if using).
8. Serve and enjoy your delicious honey lavender latte!

Chapter 9: Gourmet Coffee Recipes

RECIPE NO#88
HAZELNUT PRALINE

Ingredients:

- 1 cup of milk (dairy or non-dairy)
- 1 tablespoon of hazelnut syrup
- 1 tablespoon of praline syrup
- 1 shot of espresso or 1/2 cup of strong brewed coffee
- Whipped cream (optional, for topping)
- Crushed hazelnuts (optional, for garnish)

Instructions:

1. In a small saucepan, heat the milk over medium-low heat until it starts to steam.
2. Add the hazelnut syrup and praline syrup to the milk and whisk until well combined.
3. Brew a shot of espresso or make strong brewed coffee.
4. Slowly pour the milk and syrup mixture over the espresso or coffee, holding back the foam with a spoon.
5. Spoon the foam on top of the latte.
6. If desired, top with whipped cream.
7. Garnish with crushed hazelnuts (if using).
8. Serve and enjoy your delicious hazelnut praline latte!

Chapter 9: Gourmet Coffee Recipes

RECIPE NO#89
TIRAMISU LATTE

Ingredients:

- 1 cup of milk (dairy or non-dairy)
- 1 tablespoon of mascarpone cheese
- 1 tablespoon of chocolate syrup
- 1 tablespoon of espresso powder
- 1 shot of espresso or 1/2 cup of strong brewed coffee
- Cocoa powder (optional, for garnish)

Instructions:

1. In a small saucepan, heat the milk over medium-low heat until it starts to steam.
2. Add the mascarpone cheese, chocolate syrup, and espresso powder to the milk and whisk until well combined.
3. Brew a shot of espresso or make strong brewed coffee.
4. Slowly pour the milk and cheese mixture over the espresso or coffee, holding back the foam with a spoon.
5. Spoon the foam on top of the latte.
6. If desired, dust the top with cocoa powder.
7. Serve and enjoy your delicious tiramisu latte!

Chapter 9: Gourmet Coffee Recipes

RECIPE NO#90
PEANUT BUTTER

Ingredients:

- 1 cup of milk (dairy or non-dairy)
- 1 tablespoon of creamy peanut butter
- 1 tablespoon of chocolate syrup
- 1 shot of espresso or 1/2 cup of strong brewed coffee
- Whipped cream (optional, for topping)
- Crushed peanuts (optional, for garnish)

Instructions:

1. In a small saucepan, heat the milk over medium-low heat until it starts to steam.
2. Add the creamy peanut butter and chocolate syrup to the milk and whisk until well combined.
3. Brew a shot of espresso or make strong brewed coffee.
4. Slowly pour the milk and peanut butter mixture over the espresso or coffee, holding back the foam with a spoon.
5. Spoon the foam on top of the latte.
6. If desired, top with whipped cream.
7. Garnish with crushed peanuts (if using).
8. Serve and enjoy your delicious peanut butter cup latte!

Chapter 10: Coffee Desserts

Recipe No#91
Coffee Ice Cream

Ingredients:

- 2 cups of heavy cream
- 1 cup of whole milk
- 3/4 cup of granulated sugar
- 1/4 teaspoon of salt
- 1 tablespoon of vanilla extract
- 1/2 cup of strong brewed coffee, cooled

Instructions:

1. In a large mixing bowl, whisk together the heavy cream, whole milk, sugar, salt, and vanilla extract until well combined.
2. Add the cooled brewed coffee to the mixture and stir until fully incorporated.
3. Pour the mixture into an ice cream maker and churn according to the manufacturer's instructions, typically for 20-25 minutes or until the ice cream is thick and creamy.
4. Transfer the ice cream to a freezer-safe container and freeze for at least 2 hours or until firm.
5. Scoop and serve your delicious coffee ice cream!

Chapter 10: Coffee Desserts

Recipe No#92
Coffee Pudding

Ingredients:

- 2 cups of whole milk
- 1/2 cup of granulated sugar
- 1/4 cup of cornstarch
- 1/4 teaspoon of salt
- 2 tablespoons of instant coffee
- 2 egg yolks + 1 tablespoon of butter

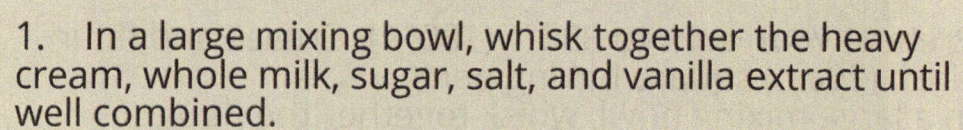

Instructions:

1. In a large mixing bowl, whisk together the heavy cream, whole milk, sugar, salt, and vanilla extract until well combined.
2. Add the cooled brewed coffee to the mixture and stir until fully incorporated.
3. Pour the mixture into an ice cream maker and churn according to the manufacturer's instructions, typically for 20-25 minutes or until the ice cream is thick and creamy.
4. Transfer the ice cream to a freezer-safe container and freeze for at least 2 hours or until firm.
5. Scoop and serve your delicious coffee ice cream!

Chapter 10: Coffee Desserts

RECIPE NO#93
COFFEE CAKE

Ingredients:

- 1 and 1/2 cups all-purpose flour
- 1/2 cup granulated sugar + 1/4 cup unsalted butter, at RT
- 1/4 cup vegetable oil + 1teaspoons baking powder
- 1/2 teaspoon baking soda +1/4 teaspoon salt
- 1/2 cup brewed coffe, cooled to room temperature
- 1/2 cup milk + 1 large egg + 1 teaspoon vanilla extract

Instructions:

1. Preheat your oven to 350°F (180°C). Grease and flour an 8-inch (20cm) square baking pan.
2. In a large mixing bowl, whisk together the flour, sugar, baking powder, baking soda, and salt.
3. In a separate bowl, whisk together the melted butter, vegetable oil, cooled coffee, milk, egg, and vanilla extract.
4. Add the wet ingredients to the dry ingredients and stir until just combined. Do not overmix.
5. Pour the batter into the prepared pan.
6. To make the streusel topping, mix together the flour, brown sugar, and cinnamon in a bowl. Add the melted butter and stir until the mixture forms small crumbs.
7. Sprinkle the streusel mixture over the top of the cake batter.
8. Bake for 35 to 40 minutes or until a toothpick inserted into the center of the cake comes out clean.
9. Allow the cake to cool for at least 10 minutes before serving.

Chapter 10: Coffee Desserts

RECIPE NO#94
COFFEE BROWNIES

Ingredients:

- 1 cup unsalted butter, melted + 2 cups granulated sugar
- 3/4 cup unsweetened cocoa powder
- 1 teaspoon vanilla extract + 1/2 teaspoon salt + 4 eggs
- 1 1/2 cups all-purpose flour
- 1 tablespoon instant coffee granules + 1/2 cup semi-sweet chocolate chips

Instructions:

1. Preheat your oven to 350°F (180°C). Grease and flour an 8-inch (20cm) square baking pan.
2. In a large mixing bowl, whisk together the flour, sugar, baking powder, baking soda, and salt.
3. In a separate bowl, whisk together the melted butter, vegetable oil, cooled coffee, milk, egg, and vanilla extract.
4. Add the wet ingredients to the dry ingredients and stir until just combined. Do not overmix.
5. Pour the batter into the prepared pan.
6. To make the streusel topping, mix together the flour, brown sugar, and cinnamon in a bowl. Add the melted butter and stir until the mixture forms small crumbs.
7. Sprinkle the streusel mixture over the top of the cake batter.
8. Bake for 35 to 40 minutes or until a toothpick inserted into the center of the cake comes out clean.
9. Allow the cake to cool for at least 10 minutes before serving.

Chapter 10: Coffee Desserts

RECIPE NO#95
COFFE CHEESCAKE

Ingredients:

- 1 1/2 cups graham cracker crumbs
- 1/4 cup granulated sugar
- 1/2 cup unsalted butter, melted

Instructions:

1. Preheat the oven to 350°F (180°C). Grease a 9-inch springform pan with cooking spray.
2. In a mixing bowl, combine the graham cracker crumbs, granulated sugar, and melted butter. Mix well, and press the mixture into the bottom of the prepared pan.
3. Bake the crust for 10 minutes, or until lightly browned. Remove from the oven and let cool.
4. In a large mixing bowl, beat the cream cheese, granulated sugar, and flour together until smooth.
5. Add the eggs and egg yolks, one at a time, beating well after each addition.
6. In a separate small bowl, mix together the sour cream, heavy cream, instant coffee granules, and vanilla extract. Add this mixture to the cream cheese mixture and beat until fully combined.
7. Pour the filling into the crust and smooth the top with a spatula.
8. Bake the cheesecake for 50-60 minutes, or until the edges are set and the center is slightly jiggly.
9. Let the cheesecake cool to room temperature, then cover and refrigerate for at least 2 hours or overnight.
10. Once chilled, remove the cheesecake from the pan and slice into desired portions.

Chapter 10: Coffee Desserts

RECIPE NO#96
COFFEE TOFFEE

Ingredients:

-- 1 cup unsalted butter
- 1 cup granulated sugar
- 1/4 cup water
- 2 tablespoons instant coffee granules
- 1/4 teaspoon salt
- 1 teaspoon vanilla extract + 1 cup chopped nuts

Instructions:

1. Line a baking sheet with parchment paper or a silicone mat.
2. In a medium saucepan, melt the butter over medium heat. Add the sugar, water, instant coffee granules, and salt, stirring constantly until the sugar dissolves.
3. Attach a candy thermometer to the side of the pan and increase the heat to medium-high. Cook the mixture, stirring occasionally, until the temperature reaches 300°F (150°C).
4. Remove the pan from the heat and stir in the vanilla extract and chopped nuts. Pour the mixture onto the prepared baking sheet, spreading it out into an even layer with a spatula.
5. Sprinkle the chocolate chips over the top of the hot toffee. Let them sit for a minute or two to soften, then use a spatula to spread the melted chocolate over the toffee.
6. Sprinkle additional chopped nuts over the top of the chocolate, if desired.
7. Let the toffee cool completely, either at room temperature or in the refrigerator. Once it is fully cooled and hardened, break it into pieces with your hands or a knife.

Chapter 10: Coffee Desserts

RECIPE NO#97
VIETNAMESE ICED

Ingredients:

- 2 tablespoons coarse ground coffee
- 3 tablespoons sweetened condensed milk
- 1 cup hot water
- 1 cup ice

Instructions:

1. Brew the coffee using a coffee filter or a French press. If using a coffee filter, place the grounds in the filter and slowly pour the hot water over them. If using a French press, pour the hot water over the grounds and let them steep for 4-5 minutes.
2. While the coffee is brewing, fill a glass with ice.
3. Once the coffee is brewed, pour it over the ice.
4. Add the sweetened condensed milk to the glass, stirring well until it is fully mixed into the coffee.
5. Enjoy your delicious Vietnamese Iced Coffee!

Chapter 10: Coffee Desserts

RECIPE NO#98
ICED CARAMEL

Ingredients:

- 2 shots of espress
- 1/2 cup milk
- 2 tablespoons caramel sauce
- 1 cup ice

Instructions:

1. Brew the espresso shots using an espresso machine. If you don't have an espresso machine, you can use a moka pot or a French press.
2. While the espresso is brewing, heat the milk in a small saucepan or in the microwave until it is hot but not boiling. If using a saucepan, stir the milk constantly to prevent it from scorching.
3. Pour the hot milk into a blender or frother and blend or froth until it is frothy and has a smooth texture.
4. Fill a glass with ice.
5. Pour the caramel sauce over the ice.
6. Add the espresso shots to the glass.
7. Pour the frothed milk over the espresso and caramel.
8. Use a spoon to gently stir the drink until the caramel is fully mixed in.
9. Enjoy your delicious Iced Caramel Macchiato!

Chapter 10: Coffee Desserts

RECIPE NO#99
ICED AMERICANO

Ingredients:

- 2 shots of espresso
- 1 cup cold water
- 1 cup ice

Instructions:

1. Brew the espresso shots using an espresso machine. If you don't have an espresso machine, you can use a moka pot or a French press.
2. Fill a glass with ice.
3. Pour the cold water over the ice.
4. Add the espresso shots to the glass.
5. Use a spoon to gently stir the drink until the espresso is fully mixed in.
6. Enjoy your delicious Iced Americano Coffee!

Chapter 10: Coffee Desserts

RECIPE NO#100
ICED MOCHA

Ingredients:

- 1 shot of espresso or 1/2 cup of strongly brewed coffee, chilled
- 1 cup of milk
- 2 tablespoons of chocolate syrup or 1 ounce of chocolate
- 1 tablespoon of sugar (optional)
- Ice cubes + Whipped cream (optional)

Instructions:

1. Brew a shot of espresso or make 1/2 cup of strongly brewed coffee and chill it in the refrigerator for at least 30 minutes.
2. In a glass, combine the chilled espresso or coffee with the chocolate syrup or melted chocolate. If you like your coffee sweet, you can add a tablespoon of sugar at this point.
3. Stir the mixture until the chocolate is completely dissolved.
4. Add ice cubes to the glass, leaving a little space at the top.
5. Pour the milk over the ice cubes. You can use any type of milk you like, but whole milk or 2% milk will give you the creamiest results.
6. Stir the mixture gently to combine the milk and coffee.
7. If you want to add whipped cream, now is the time to do it. Top the drink with a dollop of whipped cream.
8. Serve the iced mocha immediately and enjoy!

Thank You

Made in the USA
Monee, IL
03 October 2023